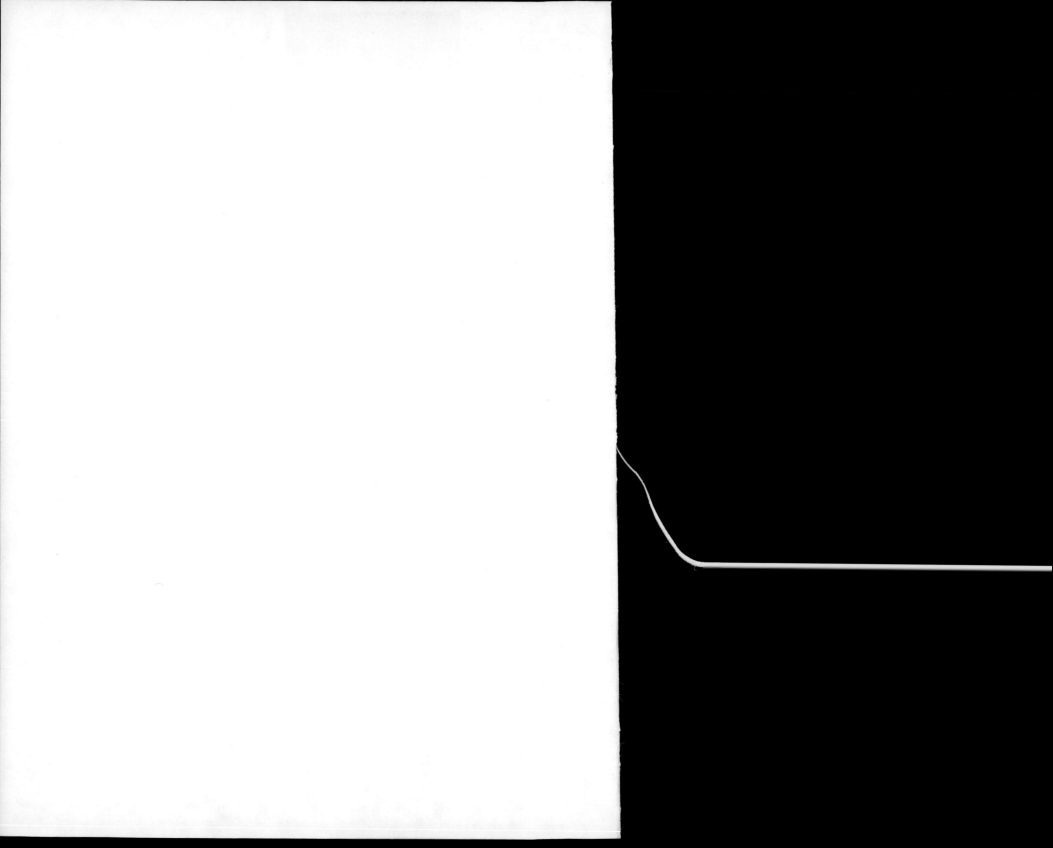

Russian Tales of Fabulous Beasts and Marvels

Lee Wyndham

Russian Tales
of *Fabulous Beasts*
and Marvels

illustrated by Charles Mikolaycak

Parents' Magazine Press

Text Copyright © 1969 by Lee Wyndham
Illustrations Copyright © 1969 by Parents' Magazine Press
All rights reserved
Printed in the United States of America
Standard Book Numbers: Trade 8193-0303-8, Library 8193-0304-6
Library of Congress Catalog Card Number: 76-77797

Book designed by Charles Mikolaycak

To the memory of my Father and Grandfather—
both of whom were master storytellers . . .

Contents

The classic stories retold here were among the best loved in old Russia, and are still treasured and told there today. I heard them as a small child in that country—from my grandparents, father and mother, and a host of affectionate aunties. Through the years my own fascination with these tales of fabulous beasts and marvels never waned. However, memory can play tricks, and so, before setting these tales on paper, I searched tenderly preserved old Russian books, checking the many variations of each story as I translated. I also consulted with scholarly emigres of old Russia—some of them now octogenarians—and of course had the happy benefit of talking each story over with my mother.

In my versions I have tried to preserve the freshness, vividness of color, the uniqueness and the cadence of phrase peculiarly characteristic of the *Skazki*—the Russian Wonder Tales—and to share my own enchantment with the young readers of today, for Wonder Tales of all nations should be part of everyone's inheritance from the past.

—Lee Wyndham

The Fold
Morristown, New Jersey

9

Foolish Emilyan and the Talking Fish

There were once three brothers who lived together in a village on the shore of the Volga River. Two of them were grown men and long married. The third one, Emilyan, was still a youth. He was a strong, good-looking fellow, with wide-set blue eyes, fair curling hair and broad shoulders. He was also bone-lazy and foolish.

The three owned a trading business left to them by their father. But it was the older brothers who ran it. Emilyan was not only simple in mind, he hated anything that even sounded like work. He spent most of his time on top of the warm ledge of the tall clay stove in the kitchen—sleeping, daydreaming or playing at knucklebones.

One day the two older brothers decided to sail down the Volga, buying and selling along the way.

Now this sounded like fun. Emilyan jumped off the

12

stove. "Why can't I go too?" he demanded.

The older men glanced at each other. Taking the foolish Emilyan along was like borrowing trouble. Yet they could never be harsh with the lad. Long ago they had promised their father always to treat him kindly.

"Well now, it's thus and it's so," they reasoned with him. "We'll be gone a long time. Someone has to stay home and take care of the house, and we think you can do that best. See to it that you act like a man. Do whatever your sisters-in-law tell you and treat them as if they were your mothers."

"There you go," grumbled Emilyan. "One minute you tell me to be the man of the house, and the next I'm a child once more—with two mothers! I don't want to stay home."

His brothers sighed. "This time you must. And if you behave yourself, we'll buy you red boots and a kaftan and a tall red hat to go with it."

"Oh, very well." Emilyan stomped off to climb on the stove ledge and sulk.

Days and weeks passed, and his brothers' wives wearied of coaxing Emilyan to help them with this and with that. Nagging didn't do much good, either. Up on the stove ledge, Emilyan ignored all their requests and entreaties. And as the weather grew bitter and the river froze over, the wives lost all patience.

13

"Emilyan!" the younger wife shouted. "Come down from the stove ledge at once and fetch us some water from the river."

"Why don't you get it yourself?" Emilyan said rudely.

"Because, foolish one, chopping a hole in the river ice is not woman's work," the older wife snapped.

"And if you don't get the water immediately, there will be nothing to cook with and therefore no dinner. And besides," the younger woman craftily added, "we will tell your brothers how lazy you've been. And then you will never get those red boots or the kaftan with the red hat to match!"

Emilyan was off that stove and away in a trice, with the large water buckets swinging on the wooden yoke over one shoulder and the axe slung over the other.

"I hate doing this," he muttered as he whacked away at the thick ice. "It's cold and nasty." WHACK—CRACK! "All day long those two women keep me at it." WHACK— CRACK! Emilyan imitated the voices of his sisters-in-law as he continued to hack out chunks of ice. "Feed the chickens, slop the pigs." WHACK—CRACK! "Clean the stable—stop your dreaming! *Pfoo!* Those women wear me out."

His breath rolled out in clouds on the cold, crisp air as he ticked off his complaints.

When the ice hole was big enough, Emilyan dipped the wooden buckets in and scooped up the water. As he thumped the second pail down beside the first, there was a swirl in the water and Emilyan saw that he had a fish in the bucket—a large, handsome pike.

"What luck!" he exclaimed. "I'll make those women cook this pike for my dinner."

"No, no!" the pike cried out in a human voice. "Put me back into the river, Emilyan, so I can return to the Caspian Sea. I'll make it well worth your while."

"Ahhh!" scoffed Emilyan. "Do you take me for a fool? How could a fish do that?"

"Surely you can tell I'm no ordinary fish," said the pike. "Have you ever heard a fish talk before?"

"Well—no," Emilyan admitted. "And you do look different from any pike I've ever seen, with your scales of silver and your back of gold—I do believe those are pearls along your spine."

"So they are," said the pike, and changed the subject lest Emilyan be tempted to keep him. "I was listening so intently to your sad complaints, there under the ice, that I didn't see your bucket coming—that's how you caught me. It isn't fair for a young fellow like you to be put upon this way. And I'll tell you what I'll do for you. Only put me back in the river and you'll never need to work again!"

"Now you interest me," said Emilyan.

"These buckets, for instance," the pike said. "They'll

be heavy as lead to carry home. I can make it so they'll take themselves home. What do you think of that?"

Emilyan fixed his eyes hopefully on the big wooden buckets, but nothing happened.

"From now on, whenever you want a piece of work done," the fish continued, "all you need to do is say, *By the Pike's command, and at my desire*—and whatever it is will be done."

"And I won't need to lift a hand?"

"Not even a finger," the pike assured him. "Now be a good fellow and let me go."

"Oh—all right." Emilyan dumped the fish back into the Volga. The water in the ice hole boiled and shot up like a geyser, then cleared and was still. Emilyan stared. "Ho, Pike, come back!" he shouted. "Tell me more about our bargain." But the ice hole remained empty. Emilyan shook his head. "I certainly let that fish talk me out of a good dinner."

He refilled the wooden bucket. It *was* heavy. And to put *two* of them on the heavy wooden yoke on his shoulder . . . He groaned and thought about the tricky pike.

It probably wouldn't do any good, but why not give the pike's command a try. He had nothing to lose.

"*By the Pike's command, and at my desire*, go home, buckets. And set yourselves up on the water shelf where you belong!"

Instantly the big buckets hung themselves on the shoulder yoke. The yoke rose in the air and floated off toward Emilyan's house.

"It works!" shouted Emilyan. "Now I won't have to! The pike spoke truly. Am I glad I didn't keep him for dinner."

Emilyan shouldered his axe and swaggered after the yoke and buckets. A neighbor who happened to be about fell in a faint at the sight. Another screeched wildly and climbed a tree. A third took one look and ran straight *through* a high snowdrift. But Emilyan's sisters-in-law were busy and didn't see a thing. As for the neighbors, after they had recovered, they decided that they had dreamed the whole thing. Not one said a word about it for fear of being called as foolish as simple Emilyan.

The next day the sisters-in-law needed firewood. "Go to the woodshed and split some," the older wife said.

Emilyan was about to argue from the comfort and warmth of the stove ledge, when he remembered the pike's promise. "Oh, very well," he agreed and jumped to the floor. This so astonished the older wife that she ran off to tell the younger one about it.

Meanwhile, Emilyan sauntered into the woodshed and said, "*By the Pike's command, and at my desire,* get yourself split, wood, and make a neat pile near the stove."

By the time the younger wife had run back to marvel

at such a willing Emilyan, the work was done. There was nothing to scold him for the livelong day. The chickens were fed, the pigs were slopped, the cows were milked and the stable was cleaned—and Emilyan was still smiling happily. It wasn't natural, but it was pleasant.

A week later, the wood in the shed was almost gone, and the older wife said, "Emilyan, you'll have to go to the forest and cut us some logs."

"Oh, no. I'm too comfortable up here on the stove ledge." Emilyan yawned, still half-asleep. "Besides, it's too cold to go out."

"It will get a lot colder if you don't get us the wood," the older wife told him crossly.

"And if you don't hurry up about it," the younger one added, "we shall tell your brothers, and you certainly will not get those red boots and the kaftan with the tall red hat to go with it."

Whoosh—foolish Emilyan was off the stove and half through the door before he remembered the pike and his promise. He turned back to his sisters-in-law, laughing. He pinched the cheek of the younger, and planted a smacking kiss on the older, and ran out the door whistling.

"Whatever has gotten into him?" the sisters-in-law asked each other.

On his way to the barn Emilyan thought, It's too bad

the pike's magic spell is supposed to be used only for *work*. Wouldn't it be fun to walk in on my sisters-in-law wearing shiny red boots, a red kaftan, and a tall red hat tilted just so! What would they threaten me with then!

He laughed as he flung two axes into the sled. And he laughed as he slapped the fat rump of the horse that usually drew it. "Not today, old friend," he told the horse, and gave it an extra measure of oats. "Today I won't need you." He sprang into the sled, pulled the shaggy bear robe about him and shouted, "Ho, sisters! Open the yard gates! I'm coming out!"

The women came running, took one look at his horseless sled and threw up their hands.

"You foolish boy, you haven't the horse!"

"Don't need it!" Emilyan yelled back. *By the Pike's command, and at my desire,* go to the forest, sled!"

The sled took off. The wives rushed to open the gate and then stood there with their mouths open. Emilyan was soon out of sight.

The way to the forest was through the village. The children, of course, were the first ones to see him coming. They screamed for their elders. Soon there was a crowd gazing on this marvel of marvels—a horseless sled speeding along by itself. And with none other than foolish Emilyan sitting inside it.

19

Now the three neighbors remembered the water buckets floating home by themselves—with Emilyan strutting behind. "He is a magician," they shouted each to the other and to the rest of the village. "And all these years we thought he was foolish!"

The simple Emilyan, however, thought nothing of the sensation he had caused. When he reached the forest, he stopped the sled, settled himself more comfortably inside the bear robe, and ordered, "*By the Pike's command, and at my desire,* axes, fell those trees; cut them up into proper lengths. Wood," he added a moment later, "pile into the cart. Neatly now!"

It was all done in minutes, and Emilyan was speeding back through the village, past the goggle-eyed village folk.

Well, a marvel like that is bound to be talked of. Soon news of Emilyan and his strange magic power reached the ears of the tsar, in his far-off marble palace on the Caspian Sea. A command from His Majesty ordered the youth to appear before him without delay.

His sisters-in-law were quite overcome by the honor. They fluttered and fussed over Emilyan, brushing out his best clothes, washing his shirt to snow-white perfection. They even polished his boots. Yet they were uneasy—knowing their foolish Emilyan.

"Mind your tongue with the tsar," they both told him. "Speak when spoken to only. Bow and scrape. Stand—don't sit in his presence. Better still, kneel! Remember, the wrath of the tsar can be fatal—and easy as not, he can part your head from your body."

"This whole thing is a nuisance," Emilyan declared. "Why should I leave my cozy stove ledge and visit the tsar? Yes, why indeed? Leave the stove ledge, that is."

"The boy's lost his mind!" the two women wailed.

"Not at all," Emilyan assured them. "And I call this visit work and a bother. Therefore, *By the Pike's command, and at my desire*, stove, take me to the tsar!"

C-RR-ACK! C-RR-UMP! The stove broke away from the house, and in the wink of an eye, had flown Emilyan into the tsar's marble palace. Softly as thistledown, the stove settled before the astounded tsar and his court.

"Ho, Tsar! You wanted to see me?" Emilyan rose to one elbow on his cozy stove ledge and looked down at His Majesty.

The tsar's pale face turned a beet purple. How dared this peasant address him at all! And how dared he look *down* on him from his ridiculous stove? For a moment the tsar considered lopping Emilyan's head off right then. But what the tsar really wanted was the secret of Emilyan's magic power.

By sending inquiries, the tsar had learned that this foolish one had come by his power through chance. And that was
absurd. A simpleton had no right to such magic; it belonged
to the tsar. How handy it would be to get things done without lifting a finger, and to travel about without horses and
carriages . . .

Young Emilyan, however, would tell the tsar nothing.
And he would not get off his stove.

The tsar fumed and fretted, then resolved to use guile.
He had a young daughter, Tsarevna Natasha. Why not have
the princess talk to this peasant? She could certainly charm
him into revealing his secret.

So Natasha was summoned and sent to Emilyan. She
stood at the foot of the stove and gazed up at him. Emilyan
paid no attention.

The princess was indignant. Everyone paid attention to
her! Kings sought her in marriage. How dared this peasant
ignore her! Then she noticed his eyes—as blue as the sea. And
she noticed his hair—so fair, soft and curly. His shoulders
were broad. Yes, he was quite handsome. She sighed.

"Oh, all right," said Emilyan. "Come on up if you must.
I'll play a game of knucklebones with you."

He gave her a hand up and they played all afternoon.
The next day they played knucklebones and shadows. And
the day after, the princess taught him a palace game, with

an ivory ball and two golden cups. Then the tsar called his daughter.

"Well, Natasha, what is his secret?"

"Oh, he's fun and he's charming!" Her eyes were like stars. "I have never met anyone like him. Father, I want to marry Emilyan."

The tsar rose a foot off his throne. "MARRY HIM! THIS STUBBORN YOUNG PEASANT?" His roar could be heard through the palace.

"Well, yes," said the princess. "It's Emilyan or no one. I've made up my mind."

The tsar fumed and fretted. He roared and he threatened. Nothing would sway her. "So be it." He sighed. But he thought, When they marry, he'll tell her about his magic power. Of course she'll tell me. Once I know his secret, I'll get rid of him promptly. She'll get over this madness.

He went to Emilyan. "You're a fine, gifted fellow," he said. "I like you. It's time that my daughter was married. And you have been chosen to wed her."

Emilyan looked horrified. "But I don't want to marry! Back home I have sisters-in-law. I've no need of a wife, too, to nag me. To be married is work and a bother. She'll want this and that and maybe wear out my magic."

The tsar had opened his mouth to roar for the guards, when the magic word *magic* was spoken. "Ah, yes," he said,

25

bottling his temper. "But you see, son, her heart's set upon it."

"Oh—well, then," Emilyan agreed. Natasha was a nice enough princess. He supposed he could learn to put up with her.

So a marriage feast was prepared, and Emilyan climbed down from his stove ledge.

What a boor! thought the tsar, watching Emilyan at the banquet table after the wedding. His manners were dreadful. He *drank* soup from his bowl with loud smacking noises. He talked with his mouth full, chomped at the meats and drank wine like water. He ignored his Natasha, while the girl sat there mooning.

The tsar became more and more mortified. "We'll be the laughingstock of the world with this bridegroom. Never mind his magic. I'll get rid of him now," he decided.

He went around to Emilyan and poured him some wine. At the same time he added a strong sleeping potion.

Not being accustomed to wine in the first place, Emilyan's head was already reeling. Now his eyes closed and he fell sound asleep.

"Seize him!" shouted the tsar to his guards. "Seal him up in a strong wooden cask and toss it into the sea as the tide goes out."

"No, no!" shrieked the princess. "What are you doing?"

26

"What I should have done long ago!" Next the tsar banished the princess to a hut on an island across from the palace. "There you will come to your senses," he told her.

But she wept day and night at the edge of the sea. The tsar could see it all from his palace windows; it was most upsetting. And it was all the fault of that stubborn Emilyan. If he had not got his magic through some ridiculous stroke of luck, and if he had not come to the palace, and if the princess had never met him . . . At this point the tsar, roaring with rage, had Emilyan's stove smashed to bits.

Emilyan, meanwhile, went bumping over the waves in his cask. When the potion wore off and he wakened, he couldn't imagine what had happened or where he was. While he was still groping about in the pitch dark, he heard a voice outside the cask.

"Emilyan, Emilyan! Hear me. I am your friend, the pike. This and this has happened to you. And your wife, the tsarevna, is crying her eyes out on a small barren island near the tsar's palace. What will you have me do?"

"Why, toss this cask on the shore at her feet and let me out of it," said Emilyan. "Though it was her idea to marry me that brought on all this trouble, I do not hold it against her. It seems she has not fared so well, either. Perhaps I can help her."

Now this was the first time in his life that Emilyan had

wanted to help someone else. And considering his own present trouble, it was even more extraordinary.

The pike smiled a big toothy smile as he bumped the cask along. "Listen, Emilyan," he said. "I am well pleased with you. You have never abused the power I gave you—not even to get yourself the red boots and the kaftan and the tall red hat to match. Because you have proved yourself worthy, you may ask for anything that your heart desires—and it shall be yours. Even wisdom."

"Ah," said Emilyan from inside the cask, "wisdom would be nice. I do get tired of being called foolish."

"From now on you won't be," the pike promised, and tossed the cask on the shore. It broke open, and the princess came running to her Emilyan.

Her beautiful robes were soiled and torn, her little face smudged and tear-stained. She did not look like a princess at all. But at that very moment Emilyan fell deeply in love with her. At the same moment, he became furious with the tsar for treating his daughter so badly.

"Dry your tears, little bride," he told her. "All will be well." He looked at her miserable hut and then over at the palace across the water. "*By the Pike's command, and at my desire,*" he said softly, and even more softly whispered his request.

"Come into our hut and rest," the princess said, already

sounding like a little wife. But when she turned toward the hut, she cried out in astonishment. In its place stood a gold and marble palace, with a full staff of servants bidding them welcome. And between it and the palace of the tsar, soared a crystal bridge of breathtaking beauty.

"This palace will be our home from now on," Emilyan told his Natasha. "And when you've a mind to visit your father, you've only to run over the crystal bridge."

To his own amazement, Emilyan found that he could forgive the tsar. After all, he had been a trial to him. And to other people too—his sisters-in-law and his brothers. But that was when I was a boy—and foolish, he thought, and put his arm round his young wife. Now I am a man—and a husband. And things will be different.

And they were. The young couple made peace with the tsar, who immediately decided that Emilyan was the best son-in-law he could possibly have. Then Emilyan sent messengers to his sisters-in-law and his brothers and they came to visit their clever and wise youngest brother. He even arranged for a great feast in his home village, in honor of his good luck and marriage.

And he had a huge cake made, and a keg filled with mead—and these he sent out to sea for his friend the pike. And Emilyan and the princess lived happily on their island, and in time ruled the tsar's kingdom wisely and well.

Ivashko and the Witch

32

In a certain village, not near, not far, not high, not low, there lived an old couple with one little son named Ivashko. They loved him so dearly, he was scarcely allowed out of their sight for fear harm might come to him.

One day Ivashko said to his parents, "I'd like to go fishing. There must be lots of fish in the lake in the woods. I could catch some for you."

"What are you thinking of! You're much too young to go to the woods by yourself," his father exclaimed. "There are all sorts of wild beasts and witches—"

"Besides, you might fall into the lake and drown!" His mother turned pale at the thought of such dangers.

But Ivashko begged and pleaded, teased and cried. So at last his father hollowed out a little boat for him from a thick log, and made him a fishing rod from a willow wand. His mother dressed him in a snow-white shirt and tied a red sash around his waist.

Both parents took him through the woods to the lake. They kissed him and blessed him. Ivashko climbed into his little dugout boat, and they pushed it into the water and went home.

It was then Ivashko discovered that his father had forgotten to make him oars. "I'll manage, anyway," he said, and sang out:

Little boat, little boat, float out a bit farther.
Little boat, little boat, float out a bit faster!

And it did. Ivashko began to fish and put his catch into the boat.

A short time later, his old mother hobbled down to the water's edge and called her son in a sweet, fond voice:

Ivashko, Ivashko, my dear son,
Float back to shore;
I've brought you food
And I've brought you drink.

Ivashko heard her and said:

Little boat, little boat, float back to shore.
That's my mother calling and I must go to her.

The boat floated to the shore. His mother gave him his food and drink and took the string of fish he had caught. Then she pushed the little boat out into the lake and went home.

Again Ivashko sang out:

Little boat, little boat, float out a bit farther.
Little boat, little boat, float out a bit faster!

The dugout floated off, and Ivashko dropped his line and began to fish. A short time later, his old father hobbled down to the water's edge and called his son in a thin, sing-song voice:

> *Ivashko, Ivashko, my dear son,*
> *Float back to shore;*
> *I've brought you food*
> *And I've brought you drink.*

And Ivashko said:

Little boat, little boat, float back to shore.
That's my father calling and I must go to him.

The boat floated to the shore. His father took the string of fish the boy had caught, gave him his food and drink, and then pushed the little boat out into the lake and went home.

Now a certain witch, named Lueda-yedka, heard Ivashko's parents calling him. Curious, she hurried to the lake and peered through the bushes. And there was Ivashko, rocking gently in his little dugout in the middle of the lake. Such a tender pink and white boy he was. Lueda-yedka's ugly mouth watered—for she was a witch who ate people. Even her name meant "people-eater." How she longed to get hold of this morsel! She crept closer to the bank and cried out in her hoarse, ugly voice:

IVASHKO, IVASHKO, MY DEAR BOY,
FLOAT BACK TO SHORE.
I'VE BROUGHT YOU FOOD
AND I'VE BROUGHT YOU DRINK.

Ivashko was so startled, he nearly fell out of his boat. *That* wasn't his father. And it certainly could not be his mother. The dreadful bray could only be the voice of a witch! He pretended that he had heard nothing and he sang out softly:

Little boat, little boat, float out a bit farther.
Little boat, little boat, float out a bit faster.
That is not my father, nor my dear mother,
But a witch who calls me
And I won't go to her.

"N'yah!" snarled the witch. "The little brat is not easily fooled. I'll call him with a voice just like his mother's, and then he'll come to shore." She gnashed her iron teeth, tightened the rope belt around her hungry middle, and hurried to the blacksmith in the village.

35

"Kuznetz! Smith!" she rasped. "Make me a voice box that will sound as sweet and fond as the voice of Ivashko's mother. If you don't, I will eat you."

Trembling with terror, the smith forged her a voice box, and when they tried it, it sounded exactly like the voice of Ivashko's mother.

Lueda-yedka rushed back to the lake, held her voice box up, and it sang out:

Ivashko, Ivashko, my dear boy,
Float back to shore;
I've brought you food
And I've brought you drink.

Now that surely is my dear mother's voice, thought Ivashko. He spoke to his little boat, and obediently it floated to shore.

Lueda-yedka sprang out from the bushes, seized the boy with one hand and the fish he had caught with the other, and loped off into the woods. No matter how Ivashko pummeled and kicked, he could not loosen her clawlike hold on him.

When she reached her crooked hut, Lueda-yedka kicked the door open, flung the fish to her scrawny cat and thrust the boy into a stout iron cage. Then she bellowed for her only daughter:

"A-LEN-KA!"

Alenka came running—the spittle image of her ugly mother. "Yes, mama? Aaahhh! *Dinner!*" she screeched, and pranced round the iron cage, poking and pinching Ivashko.

"Stop your funning. Make a fire in the stove, stupid girl," the witch shouted. "Make the oven hot as can be and roast me that brat, while I go to invite some friends for the feast."

Alenka's evil eyes glittered as she followed her mother's orders. The stove got hotter and hotter. When she opened the iron door, a great wave of heat rolled out.

"Now then, little fellow," Alenka roared happily as she yanked Ivashko out of the cage. "Come here and sit on this shovel so I can put you in properly."

Though frightened nearly out of his mind, young Ivashko used what wits were left to him. "Shovel?" He looked puzzled. "I have never yet sat on a shovel. Won't you show me how to do it?"

"It's simple," Alenka assured him. "It won't take you any time to learn. Here, you hold it and I'll show you."

But the moment she sat on the shovel, Ivashko gave it a heave, pitched her into the oven and slammed the iron door shut. He ran out of the hut, locked the door and threw away the key. Then, lickety-split, he climbed up into the top of a huge oak tree nearby.

And not a moment too soon, for the witch was return-

ing. He could hear her rough voice and hoarse laughter as she and her guests crashed through the woods.

When the ugly crowd reached the hut, Lueda-yedka pushed at the door and found it locked. She pounded and kicked it and shouted to her daughter, but of course there was no reply.

"Oh, that lazy good-for-nothing!" Lueda-yedka shrieked. "She must have gone off to amuse herself—"

At that moment an acorn fell from Ivashko's tree and hit the witch on the head.

"ALENKA!" the witch bellowed. "This is no time for games! I smell the roast burning. Get down at once!" She looked up, but instead of her daughter, saw Ivashko clinging to the topmost branches.

With a horrible cry, Lueda-yedka spun about and lunged at the door. There was a crash, and the door flew apart in a shower of splinters. The witch rushed inside to peer into the oven.

"AAAAAAAAAIE!" Shrieking, she rushed out again in a frenzy. She threw herself at Ivashko's oak and began to gnaw at the trunk. She had gnawed halfway through it when two of her iron teeth broke off with a twang.

"Don't let him get away!" she yelled to her guests and sped off to the village.

Once there, she rushed to the blacksmith. "Kuznetz! Smith!

Make me some iron teeth. If you don't, I'll eat you!"

So the smith forged two iron teeth and hammered them into her jaw, and she rushed back to gnawing the oak tree again.

Ivashko was trapped. He looked up to heaven, and there was a flock of swan-geese approaching. Ivashko stretched out his arms beseechingly.

> Oh, dear swans, oh, dear geese,
> Take me up on your wings,
> Carry me to my father's house
> Where my mother awaits me.

But the swan-geese gave no sign of having heard him. The dreadful gnawing below was like a rasping saw, and the oak tree was beginning to groan and sway. Soon it would crash to the ground. Ivashko closed his eyes and prayed. When he opened them, the flock of swan-geese had almost flown past.

And then, all at once, a great white swan swooped out of the sky and flew straight down to Ivashko. The boy grasped the bird by the neck and swung up on its back. Away they flew—just as the mighty oak fell, SMASH! on top of the witch. It squashed her quite flat—and her ugly friends with her.

The great swan carried Ivashko all through the night. As the sun rose, the boy looked down—and there was the lake, and his little boat bobbing on it. Someone had tied it up to a birch tree. And there was his father's house. The swan glided down to the thatched roof.

Ivashko slid off the broad back. Before he could thank the great bird, it soared up into the sky and was gone to catch up with the flock.

Ivashko smelled breakfast cooking and heard the sound of weeping inside the cottage.

"What *could* have happened to our dear son?" his mother was sobbing. "Where *is* my Ivashko?"

"There, there," Ivashko heard his father say. "Perhaps the lad only wandered off. You know how boys are."

"Well, sit down and eat," said the mother. "I have made a stack of pancakes, though I could scarcely see to turn them through my tears. Here's one for you, and here's one for me. One for you, one for me."

Ivashko rolled to the edge of the roof, jumped to the ground and ran into the little house. "And what about me?" he shouted. "Don't I get any?"

His parents jumped up and hugged him and kissed him and laughed and cried. Then his mother fed him and hugged him and kissed him and laughed and cried. And after that, Ivashko was able to tell them everything that had happened.

"And now that the witch is dead," he said, "and won't be up to her tricks, I'd like to go back to my fishing."

And he did.

44 When Kuzenko the Orphan found himself alone in the world, he decided to leave his home village and seek his fortune. But after three years of wandering, all he had to show for it was an old horse, a black hen and a thin wool blanket. The horse he rode—when it wasn't too lame to carry him. The hen he carried about in an old bird cage—and now and again she laid him an egg. The blanket he folded over by day and used in place of a saddle. At night he rolled himself up in it and slept on the hard ground.

One day, as he led his poor horse through a deep forest,

Kuzenko came upon a tumbledown hut, held together by a few clumps of sod. The weather was cold and dreary, and it threatened to rain before nightfall.

Kuzenko stared at the hut. "Well, it's better than nothing," he said. "Come, little hen, at least we'll be snug and dry." He looked back at his drooping nag.

"You too, old friend. We can keep each other warm in there."

So they settled down for the night.

No sooner were they asleep, than a small red fox followed her sharp nose into the hut. "Wonder of wonders," she said. "A nice plump hen, right in the middle of the great green forest. This I can't resist."

The cage proved no problem. But as the clever little fox opened the door and grasped the hen, it gave a frightened squawk and awakened Kuzenko. The next moment the hen was dead, and Kuzenko had a firm grasp on Foxie's tail.

45

"Let me go!" shrilled the fox, but Kuzenko held on all the tighter.

"I can tell by your brush—even in the dark—that you are a fox," he said. "And I'm sure as sure that you've done away with my hen. And as certainly as my name is Kuzenko the Orphan, I'll not let you go."

"I took your hen only because I was starving," the fox wailed. "Surely you know what it's like to be hungry."

"That I do," said Kuzenko. "I am hungry right now."

"Well, then," argued the fox, "since the hen is killed anyway, let us not waste it but eat it—together. I will gather some twigs, and you make a fire and roast it. And if you share the hen with me, I will reward you."

"Oh you will, will you!" Kuzenko couldn't help but admire the wily little fox. "Still, what's done is done and cannot be undone. Get the wood and I'll pluck the hen." He let go of the fox, and the creature frisked out of the hut and into the forest.

Back and forth she came, and soon they had a pile of wood, a fire burning—and the hen roasting. When the hen was eaten, the fox sat back and regarded Kuzenko thoughtfully.

"I have decided how to reward you," she announced. "I shall get you exactly what you need—a beautiful, rich wife. I have the very girl in mind, in fact, a tsarevna."

Kuzenko the Orphan threw back his head and laughed. "Dear, foolish Foxie," he chortled, "who'd have a poor fellow like me? Least of all a royal princess—a tsarevna. Ho, ho, ho! Ha, ha, ha!"

"Laugh and be happy," said Foxie. "But don't stir from this hut till I come back. Give me a week, and I promise you a tsarevna, no less!"

Of course Kuzenko didn't believe a word of this. What

is more, he never thought he'd see Foxie again. But he had no place to go anyway. There was a good patch of grass nearby for his horse, wild apples and grapes at the edge of the clearing, and all the rabbits he wanted to snare for himself. "Not to mention a roof over my head," Kuzenko told his nag as he led it out to graze. "Why, look at it all, horse! Any lovely tsarevna would find this a palace!" And he set to laughing again.

But Foxie wasted no time after she left Kuzenko the Orphan. It so happened there was a royal palace nearby which belonged to the Thunder King, Tsar Grom, and his Lightning Queen, Tsaritza Molniya. And they did indeed have a lovely daughter, of the right age to be wed. Foxie knew all this, for she had been a palace gossip for years. Now she whisked past the guards, raced through the marble halls, and straight into the royal sitting room. The tsar and tsaritza were drinking tea from a golden samovar.

Foxie skidded to a stop, bowed respectfully and sat up, bright-eyed and panting.

"Why, Foxie, dear gossip," said the tsaritza. "You look as if you've been running for miles. Have you news for us?"

"That I do," said the fox. "I've become a matchmaker. And I've found a bridegroom for your daughter. Kuzenko Sudden-Wealthy. What do you think of that?"

"What should we think?" said the tsaritza. "We have never heard of Kuzenko before. Why doesn't he come and woo the princess himself? What's the matter with him?"

"Not a thing but affairs of state," said the fox. "He has just inherited a great forest province, and he moves about it with a silk tent for a palace. Lacking for nothing in comfort, you understand. He rules over thousands of forest creatures, doing with them what he wishes, and he cannot leave just now."

"Well, then," said the tsar, between tea sips, "as a token of his love for our daughter, tell him to send us a pack of gray wolves—say, forty forties in number. And then we may consider him as a son-in-law."

"But before you go," added the queen kindly, "stop by the kitchen and have the cook feed you."

Foxie did just that—and ate and ate till she could eat no more. Then she left the palace and ran to a meadow at the edge of the deep green forest. She threw herself on the grass and, yipping happily, began to roll about and pat her bulging stomach.

It wasn't long before a gray wolf slunk out of the woods. "I see you have dined well somewhere," he remarked.

"That I have," said the fox. "And I wish I hadn't eaten quite so much—but you know the kind of table Tsar Grom and Tsaritza Molniya set for a banquet. All the animals are

still there, stuffing themselves—the bears, the sables and the ermines . . ." She stopped rolling about, sat up and looked at the wolf. "Don't tell me you weren't invited?"

The wolf shook his head. "None of us was."

"What an oversight!" cried the fox. "I'll correct it at once. You know how close I am to their Royal Majesties. Go to the woods and gather together forty forties of your gray wolf brothers. Be here tomorrow and I shall take you to the palace myself."

On the following day the wolf pack was ready and waiting. Foxie led them through the stout gates of the tsar's palace and announced to their Majesties that Kuzenko Sudden-Wealthy had sent the gray wolves to them.

The tsar and tsaritza were delighted. "Drive them into the paddock," the tsar ordered his guards. "As for you, dear Foxie, tell Kuzenko Sudden-Wealthy that we'd like just as many black bears for a present."

"But before you go," the tsaritza said kindly, "stop by the kitchen and have the cook feed you."

Foxie did just that. And then, as before, she trotted out to the meadow and began to roll about, yipping happily and patting her bulging stomach.

Soon a shaggy black bear ambled out of the woods. "It's plain to be seen you have dined well," he rumbled.

50

"That I have," said the fox. "I've just been to the tsar's banquet for the animals—there were hundreds of us there. Ermines, sables—the wolves are feasting there now . . ." She stopped rolling about and looked at the bear. "Weren't you invited?"

The bear shook his head. "None of us was."

"Just an oversight!" cried the fox. "I'll correct it at once. You know how close I am to their Majesties. Bring together forty forties of your shaggy bear brothers. Meet me here tomorrow, and I shall take you to the palace myself."

The bears were ready and waiting when Foxie came to the meadow the next day. Everything happened exactly as planned —only this time the greedy tsar said, "If your Kuzenko Sudden-Wealthy could send us this many wolves and this many bears, have him send us a gift of as many ermines and sables."

"But before you go," the kind tsaritza added, "stop by the kitchen and have the cook feed you."

Once more Foxie ate more than her fill. Once more she put on the same performance in the meadow.

This time a sable and an ermine scurried out of the woods. "Where have you been feeding, Mistress Fox?" they asked her together. "You look ready to burst."

"That I am," said the fox. "I've been feasting with the

tsar and tsaritza. You know how close I am to their Majesties. Well, I asked them to make a banquet for the forest beasts and they have outdone themselves. I took the bears and the wolves there—and they're feeding yet—but I couldn't eat another bite."

"We'd like to go, too." The sable and the ermine gazed pleadingly at the fox.

"Oh, I couldn't bother their Majesties just for the two of you," said the fox. "But I'll tell you what, if you'll gather your brother sables and brother ermines together—say, forty forties of each—and come back here tomorrow, I'll take you all to the palace myself. You'll scarcely believe what goodies await you!"

And so forty forties of sables and forty forties of ermines were presented to Tsar Grom and Tsaritza Molniya. The stockades could hold no more animals, and the tsar was well pleased.

"Now," he said, "tell this Kuzenko Sudden-Wealthy, who would be our son-in-law, to come here himself. We want a look at him—and it's time he met his bride-to-be."

"I shall do so at once," cried the little red fox.

But she came back to the palace alone the next day. "Your Majesties," she said, "my master begs your pardon. He cannot come today."

"WHAT!" thundered Tsar Grom, half-rising from his throne.

"*What!*" shrieked Tsaritza Molniya, and streaks of lightning flashed from her jeweled headdress. "How dare he refuse our command!"

"Gracious Majesties," the fox broke in hastily, "the reason Kuzenko cannot come is because he is gathering together all his treasures, in order to lay them at the feet of your daughter."

"Oh, so that's it," said Tsar Grom, and settled back comfortably on his throne.

"What a dear, thoughtful young man," the tsaritza purred, and the lightnings around her head became soft twinklings.

"Yes, indeed," Foxie agreed. "And what he'd like to borrow from Your Majesties is a corn measure."

"*Corn* measure?" The tsar and tsaritza sat bolt upright. "Whatever for?"

"Why, to measure his treasure, of course," said the fox.

"Well, take it to him," the tsar said after a puzzled glance at his wife.

Foxie returned on the morrow, bringing back the corn measure. But she had stuck a gold piece and two silver pieces to the bottom of it.

"My master bade me tell Your Majesties that he will be with you shortly, with all the riches in his possession."

"We shall welcome him gladly and arrange a splendid reception in his honor," the tsar said.

As soon as Foxie had left, the tsar turned to the tsaritza and rubbed his hands together. "What a son-in-law to have," he said. "Imagine, he cannot even count his gold and silver piece by piece but must measure it!"

"Our darling daughter shall want for nothing with a husband like that," the tsaritza murmured. "I must go to her now and tell her she is to be married."

While the preparations at the palace went apace, Foxie sped through the deep green forest to the hut where she had left Kuzenko. She found him sleeping on his threadbare blanket.

"Awake! Get up! We must hasten to the tsar's palace. You are about to meet your bride!" shouted the fox, nipping at Kuzenko's heels to get him moving faster.

"Stop that nipping!" Kuzenko kicked out at the fox. "I am in no mood for jokes."

"This is no joke," Foxie assured him. "All is as I say, but you must hurry. Tsar Grom and Tsaritza Molniya do not like to be kept waiting—not even by such a wealthy son-in-law-to-be as yourself!"

"*Wealthy!* Did you tell them that?" Kuzenko was aghast.

"Not only told it, but proved it!" Foxie laughed and as

quickly as possible told him exactly how she had managed it. "Now you see why you must come with me," she finished.

"But I've nothing to wear!" shouted Kuzenko. "I can't show up at the tsar's palace looking like this!"

"Oh you tiresome fellow," screamed the fox. "It's clear to see you've no fox-blood in your veins. Do as I say and leave the rest to me."

So Kuzenko brushed off his tattered clothes, went to the clearing and got his nag. Then he folded the threadbare blanket that he used in place of a saddle, put it on the creature's bony back and clambered on.

"Lead the way, Foxie," he said. "And I hope this adventure won't cost us our heads."

"It won't, if you use yours," she assured him.

By and by they came in sight of the palace. There was only a bridge to cross, over a deep gorge with a swift running stream.

"Stop and dismount," ordered the fox. "Drive your nag into the green meadow yonder, then come back and help me."

When Kuzenko returned, she showed him a saw she had hidden in the bushes. "Saw through the supports of the bridge," she told him.

Kuzenko shrugged and set to work. After a while he said, "Won't this make the bridge fall?" No sooner were the words out of his mouth, than the bridge cracked and plunged into

the gorge. A moment more, and the pieces were swept downstream and out of sight.

"Quickly now," said the fox, before Kuzenko could recover his breath, "take off all your clothes and throw them into the river. Roll about in the dirt and get a few scratches on you. Look exhausted. Half-drowned! Good. I'll be off now, but when I come back, you look exactly this way. Unconscious. Listen to what I say then—and your fortune will be made."

"Well," Kuzenko said to himself, "I have gone this far with the crazy fox, I might as well go further." And he lay as one dead at the edge of the river gorge.

Before long, Kuzenko heard voices, cries of dismay and the thud of running feet. Foxie reached him first and whispered fiercely, "Lie still!" just as Kuzenko was about to jump up and run for it.

"Oh my dear, dear master!" she wailed, as the tsar and tsaritza, and all their court and their soldiers and their servants, caught up with her. "See! It is just as I told you. A terrible accident. Kuzenko Sudden-Wealthy was crossing your bridge, with *all* his people and a caravan of horses loaded with *all* his treasure. And then—oh, it was terrible! Your old bridge gave way and everyone—everything—*all the treasure*—plunged into the gorge."

The whole assembly rushed to the edge of the gorge.

But not a smidgen of treasure was visible—naturally.

"Gone! All gone!" wailed Foxie. "And my poor master dead!" She rushed back to Kuzenko and gave him a poke in the ribs. "He stirs! He breathes! Do something! Save him!"

"Yes, yes, we must!" shouted the tsar. "At once. Here, take my royal robes and wrap up our dear son-in-law-to-be in them. Carry him to the palace. Oh, what a near tragedy— and on our very own bridge!" The tsar shuddered. "I trust our dear son-in-law-to-be won't hold it against us."

"Well, I don't know. He did lose everything," said the fox.

Kuzenko felt himself lifted, wrapped gently and carried to the marble palace. There he was placed on a soft bed and covered by silken sheets. It was now time to allow himself to be revived, Foxie whispered in his ear. So Kuzenko let his eyes flutter open. This was greeted by an outcry of joy.

At once servants surrounded him. They washed him, they dried him, they perfumed him and curled his hair. They asked, "What is your pleasure, Your Highness?" "What can we do for you?" "Would you care to wear this satin shirt?" "These velvet trousers?" "That gold-embroidered kaftan?" "Which jewels?" "—all from the tsar's own wardrobe."

Softly, respectfully, questions came from all sides, and Foxie guided his answers.

Soon Kuzenko Sudden-Wealthy stood transformed before a mirror, admiring the vision facing him. Truly, this was the handsomest of princes. He would have stood there posturing and preening the rest of the day, but for a sharp nip from Foxie.

"They've decided to celebrate the wedding at once," she whispered, "so that you won't be inclined to make war on the tsar because of that broken bridge. From now on, the tsar told me, half of all he possesses is yours. So there's no need to mourn the treasure that went down the river!"

"Well, that's a relief," Kuzenko answered. "And now, if my bride-to-be is all you say, I just may be inclined to forgive the tsar for the poor quality of his bridge." Kuzenko practiced looking haughtily down his nose, the way he thought a real prince might. But a nip from Foxie stopped all that nonsense.

"Come," she said. "The Royal Princess awaits!"

With his heart thudding, Kuzenko strode down one marble hall and up another. At the same time, the princess, with her heart beating wildly, was being led to meet her bridegroom.

But the moment the young people saw each other—the shy, lovely tsarevna and the handsome Kuzenko in his royal robes—they fell madly in love and thought of nothing but each other. They were married that very day and lived happily ever after—with Foxie guiding Kuzenko until he became accustomed to life at the court and the ways of princes.

The Magic Acorn

In a tiny village, at the edge of a forest, there once lived an old man and his wife in a patched-up little house called a *hata*. They were desperately poor, having sold everything they possessed to buy food to keep body and soul together. Not a chick was left in the hen yard. The pig was long gone to a more fortunate neighbor, and the cow sold so long ago, the old couple could scarcely remember ever having had one. Now there wasn't even a crumb in the cupboard.

"We'll just have to go to the woods and gather acorns," the old woman said. "If we dry them on the stove, I can grind them up into acorn flour in our old hand-mill and make bread. We might even make acorn soup to go with it."

The old man smiled at her gently through his long gray beard and patted her work-worn hand. "I'm a lucky man to have such a clever wife," he told her.

So they ate acorns—dried, roasted, boiled and baked— with never a word of complaint.

One day the old woman dropped an acorn, and it rolled under the floorboard covering the small cellar.

The acorn sprouted and started to grow. In no time at

all the sprout had grown as high as the floorboard.

"*Dedushka*—dear old man," said the wife, "cut a hole in the floorboard. Let the little oak grow. When it is a tree, we won't need to go to the forest for acorns. We'll pick them right here from our own *hata.*"

"How clever of you to think of it," the old man said and cut the floor.

The oak tree grew and grew, and soon it had reached the ceiling. The old man made a hole in the ceiling. Next he made a hole in the roof. The tree continued to grow until it reached all the way to the sky.

"Surely there must be acorns up there now," the old woman said. "Ours are all gone."

"I'll climb up and see," the old man told her.

He took a sack and climbed and climbed and finally reached the topmost branches in the sky. But there were no acorns on the tree. Instead he found a small banty cock, with a golden crest and rich glossy feathers, roosting in the branches. Next to the banty cock hung a hand-mill, sky blue on the outside and golden inside.

The old man scratched his long gray beard and thought about it. Since this was their oak tree, the rooster and the hand-mill must belong to them, too. *Hap!* He grabbed the pretty rooster and stuffed it into the sack. Then he put the hand-mill in and climbed down the tree into the *hata.*

"There were no acorns up there," he told the old woman regretfully. "But there was this and this." He set the sky blue golden hand-mill and the little cockerel on the table. "What shall we do? What shall we eat?" And he gazed down at the little cock.

"Well, not the pretty cock, surely." The old woman touched the golden crest and stroked the glossy feathers.

She reached out for the mill and gave the handle a turn. All at once there was a pancake on the table. At the next turn a *pirog*—meat cake—slid out. The old people could not believe their eyes—or their luck. They took turns cranking the little mill, laughing and crying—and eating the good things. They fed the banty cock, too, and it flapped its wings and crowed happily.

The old couple marveled. "To think all this came from our own little acorn!"

The old woman prudently made extra meat cakes and pancakes and stored them in the cupboard—just in case things did not go so well later. But she need not have worried. Whenever they were hungry, the little mill provided the food.

One day a wealthy merchant—a *barin*—happened to be riding by the little hut. He stopped for a drink from the well, and the kind old woman offered him a pancake and a *pirog* from the hand-mill.

The *barin*'s eyes popped when he saw the marvel.

"Sell me the mill, *babushka*," he said. "I'll pay well for it."

The old woman shook her head. "With poor people money does not roost. It takes wings and flies away," she said. "But the hand-mill will feed my old man and myself the rest of our lives."

The *barin* scowled and went his way. That night the marvelous hand-mill was stolen.

The old man and his woman were sorely grieved. But the little cock with the golden crest stretched himself, flapped his wings and spoke to them in a human voice. "Grieve not, *dedushka* and *babushka*. I will go after the thief." And he flew away, straight to the *barin*'s courtyard.

"Ku-ku-RE-koo!" he shouted. "*Barin, barinin,* give us back our sky blue golden hand-mill!" Over and over he crowed and shouted, until the thief heard him and came out on his balcony. His face was red and his eyes blazing.

"Throw this insolent fellow into the well!" he shouted to his servants and slammed back into the house.

The little cock with the golden crest was caught and flung down a deep well. He immediately began to chant, "Little beak, little beak, drink the water. Little mouth, little mouth, drink the water!" And he drank all the water in the *barin*'s well.

With a shake and a shout he flew out of the well, straight to the *barin's* balcony. There he perched and crowed, "Ku-ku-RE-koo! *Barin, barinin,* give us back our sky blue golden hand-mill!"

The furious *barin* called the kitchen maid and ordered her to throw the rooster into the stove. The little cock was caught and thrust into the fire. Immediately he began to chant, "Little beak, little beak, pour water. Little mouth, little mouth, pour water!" *Pshish-sh-sh* . . . out went the fire. Out flew the little cock, straight into the great hall, where the *barin* was entertaining guests.

"Ku-ku-RE-koo!" he crowed, louder than ever. "*Barin, barinin,* give us back our sky blue golden hand-mill!"

The guests leaped to their feet at sight of the marvelous little talking cock with the golden crest and glossy feathers. They stared at the *barin* and then at the sky blue golden hand-mill he'd been showing off to them. But when the little cock began to swoop over the table, they pushed back their chairs and took to their heels, fearing the furious little creature might peck their eyes out.

"Wait! Come back!" The *barin* ran after his guests.

The little cock with the golden crest swooped down, snatched up the sky blue golden hand-mill and flew back to the old man and old woman. And they were never hungry again as long as they lived.

The Firebird

1

In the splendid gardens of the old Tsar Vladislas, there grew all kinds of rare trees and plants. But this old king's favorite was a small apple tree which bore golden apples. Every morning the tsar strolled in his gardens, and at ten precisely he always walked around the small apple tree and counted the golden apples. There were always one hundred—exactly.

One day the tsar counted his apples once . . . twice . . . three times. Something was terribly wrong. There were only ninety-nine on the tree! The old tsar's attendants thought the apple might have fallen and rolled away. They dropped to their hands and knees and searched the whole garden. It was not to be found anywhere.

The next day another apple was gone, and the next and the next! Four apples vanished. The tsar was in a rage. "Something must be done—and at once!" he shouted. "Summon my sons to my chambers."

The three young princes—Dimitri, Vasily and Ivan were practicing knightly arts in the courtyard. Still clad in their armor, they hastened to their father.

"My beloved children," he said, "someone is stealing my golden apples. I want the thief caught. Whoever captures him, shall have half of my kingdom while I live, and all of it upon my death."

As one, the young men knelt before him; as one, they vowed to catch the thief.

"Very well. But it is only fair that you should try to do so in turn," the old tsar said. "Tsarevitch Dimitri, you are the eldest. Therefore you take the first watch."

That night Dimitri settled himself under the apple tree. Soft winds blew, the nightingale sang, Dimitri fell asleep—and another apple vanished.

The old tsar was furious. "See that *you* do better," he commanded his second son.

Tsarevitch Vasily settled himself under the apple tree with the best of intentions, but he, too, fell asleep—and another apple vanished.

"*Six* golden apples—gone!" roared the tsar. "Can't I trust anyone to catch the thief?"

"I have not yet had my turn," Ivan Tsarevitch, the youngest, reminded the tsar.

He went off to his room and took a long nap. Thus refreshed, he was able to stay awake despite the soft lulling breezes and the sweet songs of the nightingale. Even so, it wasn't easy.

One hour went by . . . another . . . and another . . . and another. . . . The prince was stifling a yawn when all at once the whole garden was filled with brilliant light. A bird, with radiant feathers of scarlet and gold and eyes like crystal, flew into the garden and perched on a branch of the precious apple tree. It was the fabulous Firebird!

Before the astonished prince could move, the Firebird picked off an apple and spread her dazzling wings for flight. Ivan Tsarevitch made a mighty leap. But the bird rose into the air with a piercing cry. And all that remained in his hands was the luminous red-gold feather from her long, sweeping tail.

Tsar Vladislas and his elder sons came to the garden at

dawn, expecting to find Ivan Tsarevitch asleep. Instead, his youngest son held out the dazzling feather, saying, "Dear father, this came from our thief, the Firebird! I'm sorry I could not catch her, but I gave her such a fright, I don't think she'll be back."

"Well done, my son!" the tsar exclaimed.

The older brothers glared resentfully at the youngest. Still, since Ivan Tsarevitch had not been able to catch the thief, he was welcome to their father's praise. At least he would not get the kingdom.

The old tsar was enchanted with the dazzling feather. In a dark room it shone like the gold sun itself. For hours the old man sat with the shutters shut and the drapes drawn and gazed at his treasure. Even the golden apples remained uncounted. At last the old tsar could contain his desire no longer. He summoned his elder sons to him.

"Dimitri, Vasily—I must have the Firebird. I charge you with this quest. Go forth without delay. Find her and bring her to me—alive. And that which I promised before shall go to him who delivers the bird into my hands."

The two brothers stole a glance at each other. When the tsar commands, all must obey; but the same thought crossed their minds: If that eager young nuisance, Ivan Tsarevitch, had not snatched the feather from the Firebird, this bothersome quest would not be their problem now.

They had no idea where the Firebird could be found—and cared less. Jousts, hunts and banquets were much more to their liking. They glared balefully at their youngest brother as they set off.

No sooner were they away, than Ivan Tsarevitch was begging his father to be allowed to go also. At first the old man refused. "I cannot have all my sons gone at the same time," he said. But at last, so great was his desire to have the Firebird, he yielded to the youth's entreaties. Surely one of his three sons would succeed in finding and capturing the glorious creature.

2

Ivan Tsarevitch immediately selected a roan horse from the stable and set off in the direction that the Firebird had flown. He rode far and wide, high and low. Weeks passed and months, until he came to a broad green meadow. Thinking to let his horse graze, he dismounted, and in that instant his horse turned to stone! Dismayed, the prince looked about and saw an enormous gray wolf. Though the creature was on all fours, it stood half as high as a man.

"This meadow is mine," growled Gray Wolf. "Neither man nor beast is permitted here. Be off, or I'll turn you to stone also."

74

Ivan Tsarevitch gazed at his stone horse regretfully. He pulled down the knapsack, slung it over one shoulder and set off on foot across the wide meadow. He trudged that whole day without stopping and was still in the meadow when such weariness overcame him, he had to sit down and rest.

No sooner had he stretched out his legs and sighed with relief, than the huge wolf stepped out of the tall grass.

"Stay where you are, young man," the wolf told him. "I shall not harm you. I'm sorry about your horse, but such is my custom. After what happened to him, I thought you'd turn back and go home. Yet you have pressed on, so your quest must be urgent—and I admire your courage. Tell me who you are and what is your errand."

So Prince Ivan told him his story, meanwhile sharing his bread, meat and mead with the huge furry creature. Thereafter, the wolf regarded the young prince even more kindly.

"What's done cannot be undone," said the wolf. "At least not right now. And in any event, I can be more useful to you than a horse. Come! Sit on my back, Ivan Tsarevitch. Hold on tightly, and I shall take you to your destination at the world's end."

The prince mounted the wolf, grasped his thick ruff, and the creature sped off more swiftly than any horse. At times

the prince was convinced they were flying. They traveled that night and the next day. At nightfall, the wolf stopped at the foot of a stone wall surrounding an enormous black castle.

"Behind that wall is a garden," Gray Wolf said. "In that garden is a silver tree. On the tree hangs a golden cage. In that cage is the Firebird—sound asleep and yours for the taking."

"But to whom does she belong?" the prince asked, for he had not thought of stealing the bird. Fighting for her perhaps, or buying her, but not stealing.

"Ah, well, she belongs to Kostchey the Deathless—a cruel wizard," Gray Wolf answered. "It was he who sent her to steal the gold apples from your father, the tsar. That is how Kostchey gets all his treasures—by theft and by craft—and he does not always treat what he gets kindly. He's a dangerous enemy. Against him the usual weapons are useless. He can only be conquered by magic. You need not worry, however. Right now he is far away, and if you do as I tell you, all will go well for you."

This put a different light on the matter.

"Waste no time," Gray Wolf continued. "Hasten to the silver tree. Take the bird, but do not take the golden cage. If you do, you shall instantly be caught by Kostchey's guards."

77

Ivan Tsarevitch climbed over the wall. He found the Firebird at once, for all around her she cast a dazzling circle of light. He opened the golden cage door carefully, took out the sleeping bird and tucked her under his arm. He was halfway back to the wall when he thought, How awkward this is. Why not take the cage? Where will I put the bird otherwise?

He returned to the silver tree and slipped the Firebird back in her cage. The moment he lifted the cage, the golden wires set up such a twanging. They awakened the bird, who set up such a screeching. This awakened Kostchey's guards who came running. The guards seized Ivan Tsarevitch, threw him on the ground and tied him up like a sausage. Then they dragged him behind the stable and dumped him on the damp earth. "You'll wait here till our master returns and tells us what to do with you," they said.

It was too late to regret not following Gray Wolf's advice, but regret it he did. And no sooner had Ivan Tsarevitch thought of him, than Gray Wolf appeared before him.

"A fine thing you have brought on yourself," said Gray Wolf. "Lie still while I gnaw the ropes through."

When the prince was free, the two started to creep past the rear of the stable. But there was a window, and Prince Ivan couldn't resist taking a peek at Kostchey's horses.

"Ah, Gray Wolf, look here," the prince whispered. "Now

there is a horse fit for a king! Milk-white, with a gold mane and tail and four golden hoofs shod with diamonds."

The wolf looked and nodded. "The horse is fit for a king," he agreed. "But it was stolen from the young queen, Tsaritza Irena the Fair. The horse won't obey Kostchey the Deathless and, as you can see, he's been treating it badly."

The prince saw the whip marks and his heart went out to the beast.

"I suppose you'd like to rescue the creature," the wolf added drily, "and the young queen who pines in yon tower."

"What, is she here also?"

"That she is, for Kostchey stole her away from her own splendid kingdom—horse and all—one day when she was out riding. He wants to make Irena his bride, but the fair one cannot abide the ugly old wizard."

"Well, let us rescue her then!" the prince stated grandly.

The wolf laughed. "Isn't that fine talk for a youth who lay trussed up like a sausage only minutes ago!"

The prince hung his head. When he spoke again, it was in a tone much more humble. "You will help me, won't you?"

"That I will, Ivan Tsarevitch. But you must do as I say —and first things first—so that all will go well for you. It is noon now, and the stable grooms are drowsing. They'll sleep soundly enough. Climb in through this window. Go up boldly to the queen's horse, grasp the velvet halter and lead the creature out through the stable door. But under no account touch anything else."

3

The prince climbed in through the window, walked freely among the sleeping grooms, and took hold of the milk-white steed by its velvet halter. As he led it away, he noticed the magnificent jeweled bridle hanging outside its stall.

"This must belong to the queen's horse," the prince said to himself, and reached for the bridle.

The moment he touched it, a thunderous din arose. The grooms awakened, leaped to their feet and saw at once what was happening. Seizing the prince, they rushed him outdoors and pushed him into a deep bear pit.

"We shall bring you a bear to keep you company down there," they shouted.

Alas, thought the prince, this is surely the end of me. If only I had followed Gray Wolf's advice.

The moment he thought of him, that moment Gray Wolf appeared.

"A fine thing you have brought on yourself," grumbled the wolf. "But I will save you—"

Before the wolf finished speaking, a brown bear tumbled

into the pit and sat there, quite dazed. The grooms, peering in over the edge, saw the wolf there as well.

"Aha, young fellow," they called down to Prince Ivan, "you certainly do not lack for company. And with company like that, you're not likely to give our Master Kostchey any further trouble." They laughed coarsely and went away.

"Look here," the wolf said to the bear, "we'll need your help to escape, and then we'll get you out, too. First let us spatter the pit with blood and litter it with bits of fur and pieces of Ivan Tsarevitch's clothing."

While the prince tore pieces out of his tunic, the wolf bit himself on the leg and let the blood drip as he ran around the pit. The bear did the same. After that, the brown bear stood tall and the wolf climbed up on his shoulders. Ivan Tsarevitch climbed up over both of them and sprang out of the pit. The wolf leaped out next. And he and the prince reached down and pulled out the bear, which lumbered over the castle wall and ran off into the deep forest.

"Now," said the wolf, "next time the grooms peer into the pit they will see the blood, the wolf and bear fur, and your torn clothing. They'll think that either I or the bear ate the other two and escaped himself. And that will be the end of it. But now let us get over the wall and hide."

When they were safely away, the prince said in one breath, "How can I thank you?" and asked with the next,

"And now what about Tsaritza Irena the Fair? When shall we rescue her?"

"All in good time, Ivan Tsarevitch," Gray Wolf answered. "You haven't forgotten the Firebird and the milk-white steed with the gold mane and tail and the four golden hoofs shod with diamonds? You'll not want to leave them to Kostchey the Deathless?"

"Certainly not," said the prince. "And this time I shall do exactly what you tell me."

"Very well, then. Right now I want you to rest, for tonight there is much work to be done."

The prince rested till dark. Then he climbed over the wall, took the sleeping Firebird from her cage and brought her to Gray Wolf. The wolf tied her up with a strip of silk he had torn from Prince Ivan's sash and hid her in the bushes near the castle wall.

"Now go back and get us the horse," Gray Wolf directed. "And this time stop by the tackroom and pick up the *first* saddle and bridle you see."

Again Prince Ivan did exactly as he was told. The beautiful steed allowed itself to be saddled and bridled and led from the stable. Once outside, the prince leaped into the saddle, and almost before he knew it, the horse had soared over the wall.

Gray Wolf tied the horse to a tree in a hidden place

near the castle wall. "Now," he said, "it is time to rescue Irena the Fair—and that will require both of us."

Quietly, swiftly the two scaled the wall. They ran into the castle and up one thousand high, narrow steps. These led straight up, without a turn, into the East Tower where the lovely tsaritza was kept.

When the prince opened the door to her chamber, he thought he had stepped into Kostchey's treasure house. Moonlight, streaming in through the tower windows, shone on caskets of jewels—emeralds, rubies, diamonds, rare topaz and precious white jade. There were piles of brocades and silks, bolts of velvet and satin. Trays glittered with necklaces, bracelets and brooches. Prince Ivan glanced questioningly at the wolf.

Gray Wolf shrugged. "No doubt these are gifts from Kostchey—stolen for his bride-to-be."

The gifts appeared to have been pushed aside—except for one very large tray near the curtained bed of Irena the Fair. The prince looked at the tray once—and again. Seven bright golden apples gleamed in the moonlight! These could be none but his father's—the ones stolen by the Firebird at Kostchey's command.

At that moment Gray Wolf parted the bed curtains—and all thought departed from the head of Ivan Tsarevitch. Before him lay such a beauty that his mind reeled. In the moonlight

Irena's fair skin glowed like alabaster. Her raven black hair was a soft cloud on the pillow. Her rosy lips were enchanting. And the fair queen was much younger than the prince had supposed. In fact, she was scarcely more than a girl!

Gray Wolf nudged the prince quite urgently. "Stop staring. We've no time to waste," he reminded him. "And she will not waken to be of any help to us whatsoever. She's been given a powerful potion and may sleep on for days. Place her on my back and tie her down with the silken hangings from around her bed. I will carry her out, and do you follow promptly."

The prince tied Irena on tenderly, and the wolf was ready to go when the prince said, "Wait!" He had remembered the seven golden apples.

He turned back, snatched them up from the tray and stuffed them inside his shirt. No sooner was the last apple tucked away, when a din arose in the castle. Shouting guards rushed up the steep tower stairway.

"Now you've done it!" the wolf cried. "And just when I thought you had learned your lesson."

The prince looked at the black-uniformed guards storming up single file and laughed. "I may have done it, but I may also undo it!" he shouted, and leaped in front of the wolf.

When the first guard was within arm's reach, the prince

lunged and pushed the man hard in the chest. The fellow fell backward, knocking over the soldier behind him, who knocked over the third, who knocked over the fourth, who knocked over the fifth—and so on and so on, until the whole line fell over backward like a row of dominoes.

"Now—run!" the prince shouted, and Gray Wolf loped over the line of helpless guards, with the prince close behind.

Before the guards could recover, the prince, the wolf and the sleeping Irena were over the wall. And there were the horse and the Firebird, waiting where they had been hidden earlier. The prince lifted Irena up on the milk-white steed. The wolf slung the trussed-up Firebird over on his back— and away they sped through the night.

When they paused to rest, the wolf said, "Ivan Tsarevitch, would you mind telling me, what was it that you couldn't resist taking *this* time?"

"Why, my own dear father's golden apples," the prince answered. "They were right there, by the bedside, in a great big tray, as if Kostchey expected to have many more of them!"

At the word "Kostchey" the Firebird screeched, and Irena the Fair stirred and moaned.

"There, there," said Ivan Tsarevitch soothingly. "You are safe now, dear Queen," and the fair one grew quiet.

But they were not safe at all.

It so happened that Kostchey had returned to his castle at the world's end. He rode in just at dawn that very day and found all in confusion. The Firebird was gone. The milk-white steed with the gold mane and tail, and the four golden hoofs shod with diamonds had vanished. Worst of all, Irena the Fair had disappeared. Hysterical guards babbled of an enormous gray wolf which had carried her off from her chamber. Kostchey shrieked with rage.

When he further discovered that the seven golden apples had vanished, he stood frozen in fury, then exploded in howls and bellows. "You are all blind fools!" he roared, and rushed from the castle, his black cloak streaming behind him.

Eyes flaming, and grinding his teeth, Kostchey leaped on his coal-black horse and spurred it cruelly into a furious gallop. Over the wall he flew in pursuit of Irena the Fair, the golden apples, the Firebird and the milk-white steed.

4

At that moment, halfway back from the world's end, Gray Wolf laid his ear to the ground. "Prince Ivan," he said, "I hear galloping hoofbeats that make the earth tremble. That can only be Kostchey the Deathless—and he can only be after us. Let us be off!"

Away they sped over hills and valleys, through forests

and plains. But Kostchey pursued them, drawing closer and closer. As they were crossing a steppe that stretched flat for miles on all sides, Kostchey caught sight of them and spurred his black horse all the harder.

"Stop! Thieves!" he shrieked. "You shall pay with your lives when I catch up with you!"

"And he may do just that," the wolf said. "I am weary. Your horse, Prince, has been stumbling. Perhaps if I leave the Firebird behind, it will slow down Kostchey's pursuit."

"No, don't do that!" the prince cried. "Run on ahead. I may be able to save us." He groped inside his shirt and took out a heavy gold apple. When Kostchey drew nearer, Prince Ivan turned, took aim and hurled the gold apple with all his strength. He hoped to strike Kostchey so hard, the wizard would fall from his horse.

But Kostchey reached out, caught the apple and laughed like a demon as he stuffed it into his saddlebag.

Once more the prince hurled a gold apple. Again Kostchey caught it.

Four more times Ivan Tsarevitch tried to strike Kostchey down. Each time the wizard caught the apple, put it in his saddlebag and galloped ahead all the faster.

I have only one apple left, Ivan Tsarevitch thought sadly, and this one seems so much lighter in weight than the others—as if it were hollow. Well, here goes! He turned

in the saddle and hurled it with all his might.

The apple flew through the air, struck Kostchey full in the forehead—and shattered into a thousand splinters! With a piercing shriek, Kostchey fell from his horse—stone-dead. His black steed instantly turned into dust, leaving nothing but its saddling behind. The horse had been made through Kostchey's magic and could not exist without him.

At that very moment the Firebird sang—and Irena awakened. Quite naturally, she was terrified to find herself on a horse with a stranger, in the midst of a wide steppe. Being a queen, every inch, she neither screamed nor wept, even though her lips quivered. Instead, with cool dignity, she demanded, "What is the meaning of this? Set me down at once!"

The prince did so immediately. Leaping from the horse, he introduced himself and Gray Wolf and told the young queen all that had happened. "And we rescued not only Your Royal Majesty," the prince said, "but as you see, your own noble steed as well."

At that, Irena the Fair threw her arms around the neck of the milk-white horse and wept with joy. When she lifted her head again, the prince said, "We have also taken the Firebird, for she was stealing the golden apples from my father's favorite tree."

"Ah, yes, the Firebird," the queen murmured, her voice like music. "You may safely release her now from the silken strip that binds her. She will not fly away."

The prince did so, and after shaking her dazzling plumes out, the bright bird rose in the air and settled herself on his shoulder.

"See? Did I not tell you?" The young queen laughed—enchantingly, the prince thought. "The bird is grateful to you, Ivan Tsarevitch. Kostchey was a cruel master. He made her fly thousands of miles to steal your father's golden apples. He thought that they were the Apples of Life—and he intended to live forever. That is why he called himself Deathless. Yet one of those apples caused his death. His fate must have been sealed inside it. You have done well, good Prince."

Ivan Tsarevitch would have basked in her smiles forever, but the wolf *harrumped* loudly and huffily. The prince was not giving him one bit of credit for all that had been accomplished. Still, a young man in love, as the prince obviously was, could not be held to account. More gently the wolf said, "Should we not be getting on?"

"Yes, indeed," agreed the prince, "as soon as I recover my father's own golden apples from Kostchey's saddlebag. All but the seventh apple—and that one was well spent!"

When the prince returned, he had the six golden apples once more inside his shirt. He leaped back on the milk-white steed and lifted the young queen before him. With the Firebird still perched on his shoulder, they rode off.

When they reached the green meadow that was the wolf's province, the gray beast gave a whistle. The roan horse which had been turned to stone came to life, but the prince never saw it. His eyes were on the queen in his arms, and from time to time he buried his face in the cloud of her raven black hair. As for Irena the Fair—she looked more like a young girl in love than a queen with a kingdom to rule.

"You've no need of me now, Ivan Tsarevitch," the wolf called as the couple rode past, "but I shall remain your friend. And when you think of me, I shall return to your side. Follow them!" he ordered the now-restored horse, and it trotted obediently after the royal pair.

5

Meanwhile, at the palace of Tsar Vladislas there was sorrow. The two older princes—Dimitri and Vasily—had long since returned. They gave awesome accounts of the terrors and dangers that they had encountered in their fruitless quest of the Firebird. Though the old tsar regretted the dangers, he was disappointed. He still longed for the fabulous Firebird. Perhaps Ivan Tsarevitch would bring it.

But as days turned into weeks and there was no sign at all of his youngest, the old tsar feared the worst. Prince Ivan would never return. "And all because of my greed for the Firebird," he moaned.

And then, on the day that he'd ordered official mourning for Ivan Tsarevitch, and the palace courtyards were draped in deep purple, joyous trumpets suddenly sounded. In through the gates rode the young prince himself, on a prancing white steed, with a beautiful maiden riding before him. A glittering bird was perched on his shoulder—and his roan horse was frisking behind.

"The prince has returned! Ivan Tsarevitch is back! *Hoorah! Hoorah! Hoorah!*" everyone shouted.

The old tsar ran to the courtyard, followed by his two older sons. Such greetings, such questions, such tears and such joy as followed are past all description. At last the tsar said, "Dearest son, you've not only found the fabulous Firebird—and my golden apples, but you've found a maid for yourself! And that horse! It's fit for a king!"

"The maid is a queen, Tsaritza Irena the Fair," the prince told his father. "The horse is her own favorite steed —but the Firebird is yours."

"And my kingdom is *yours!*" the tsar announced happily. "Half of it now and the rest when I die—as I promised."

Ivan Tsarevitch glanced at his brothers, saw their red faces and angry looks, and held up his hands. "No, my dear father. My brothers also went in quest of the Firebird. It was no fault of theirs that they did not find her. I, too, would have failed, were it not for the aid of the good Gray Wolf—" The prince looked about, for the first time aware that the wolf was not with him. "Gray Wolf, my dear friend, where are you?" he called in a loud voice.

Instantly the huge beast appeared at his side, looking vastly pleased at being remembered.

"It was Gray Wolf who took me to the world's end and Kostchey's black castle. It was he who advised me in all things—and saved my life many times. So really, I would be unworthy if I were to take a kingdom so won. Divide it between my brothers, dear father. As for me—" he turned to Irena the Fair, "the young queen has consented to make me her husband. We shall marry at once, with your kind per- mission, and set off for her kingdom which has long lain neglected. I will rule there with her—justly and well, with my friend Gray Wolf to help me."

And so it was done. Tsar Vladislas' palace was stripped of the hangings of mourning. In their place rainbow silks fluttered high in the breeze. A great feast was prepared and guests invited from miles around. Ivan Tsarevitch and Irena the Fair were married with much pomp and rejoicing.

And the Firebird flew freely about the palace and court- yard and Tsar Vladislas' gardens, never once touching the golden apples.

Russian Names and Words and How to Say Them . . .

Alenka   a-LEN-ka

Babushka   BA-bu-shka (old woman or grandmother)

Barin   BA-rin (wealthy man, merchant, or nobleman)

Barinin   ba-ri-NIN (same as Barin)

Dedushka   DE-du-shka (old man or grandfather)

Dimitri   di-MIT-ri

Emilyan   emil-YAN

Hata   HA-ta (hut, very small house)

Irena ee-REE-na

Ivan ee-VAN

Ivashko ee-VASH-ko

Kostchey kost-CHAY (half-demon half-warlock, a powerful wizard. So skinny he looks like a walking skeleton. Name derived from *kost,* meaning bone.)

Kuzenko KOO-zen-ko

Kuznetz kuz-NETZ (smith)

Lueda-yedka lieu-da-YED-ka (people-eater)

Molniya MOL-ni-ya (lightning)

Pirog pi-ROG (large yeast dough cake, made in rectangular pan. May be filled with meat, cabbage, chopped liver.)

Pirojki pee-roj-KI (small yeast dough cakes, three or four inches long, shaped to a point at each end. Filled as for pirogs; sweetened cheese or any fruit may also be used.)

Samovar sa-mo-VAR

Tsarevitch tsa-RE-vitch (prince)

Tsarevna tsa-REV-na (princess)

Tsaritza tsa-RIT-za (queen)

Vasily va-SEE-ly

Vladislas vla-dis-LAS